YOU ARE GOOD ENOUGH!

DON'T DOUBT WHO GOD HAS CALLED YOU TO BE

TENDO SERUKENYA KIMULI

Dear Mawarda,

Thank you for your support! I pray God continues to guide you in all you do!

With love from

Tendo

CONTENTS

ACKNOWLEDGEMENT

When I was 16 I was told that I wasn't good enough to take English Literature as a GCSE subject because writing and analysing text were not seen as strengths of mine. 5 years later I began to write my first book and seeing it published is simply a testament of God's goodness in my life and one of the things that can happen when we trust God with the desires of our hearts. At moments, I felt uncomfortable about actually bringing this project to completion simply because of my age (I was 23 around this time) and the fact that I felt that this type of content would be better delivered by those who are far older than I am. Despite that, here we are with the finished product and my prayer is that it serves as a great source of encouragement for you as a reader.

I want to thank my parents Paul and Grace Serukenya Kimuli for how they've raised me. Rebuking me when I needed it and loving me when I didn't ask for it. Thank you for always being supportive of all the things that I've done. I love you.

Shoutout to my three younger sisters, Sanyu, Suubi and Mirembe. You man are lit still! I'm grateful for the fact that we all get along with each other and I want to thank you guys for always gassing up the work that I do. Love you guys!

A special thanks to my uncles Ken Serukenya, Jonathan Kamya and Alex Jakana for being men that I've always been able to look up to and go to for support and guidance in times when I've needed it the most. Thank you to Pastor Lincoln Serwanga for supporting and believing in my vision to help get this book published and a very big thank you to Roxanna Kazibwe and everyone at the WriteNow House in Uganda for helping make my dream a reality!

Rest in peace to jjajja omwaami (grandfather) Henry Wassanyi Serukenya. Thank you for leaving behind a legacy that I am immensely proud to carry on.

1

MY STORY

"Life inspires people, you just affi tell it right" –
Karl Lokko

I t was around 2018. I was studying Economics at Loughborough University, and I had enrolled in a "Developing Leaders" session at Junction Church under the lead pastor (at the time), Pastor Roy Todd. During that time, I remember hearing something he said that stayed with me for quite a while: that we tend to spend the majority of our adult lives trying to get over what happened during the first eighteen years. A lot of the trials and challenges that we face during our adolescence are like a seed that is planted and takes root into our being, hidden in the soil of insecurity and fertilised through the façade of having everything together. We all have our own story and a message to share about who we are.

Upon reflection of my own childhood and adolescence, I am certain that one thing that constantly echoed in my mind without me even realising was that I was not good enough. This is a fear that I am actively working hard to overcome, and this is what this book is about. It is my heartfelt attempt to show you that you too can overcome your own insecurities and fears and know that you are in fact good enough. I have tended to doubt myself a lot in the past and really question whether I actually am good enough for what I believed God has called me to do. Areas of my life where I know God has blessed me with a particular gift or ability to do something to an excellent standard, include creative outlets such as music, writing, podcasting and sport (hockey) and the doubts I've had about myself have had a large impact on the amount of faith that I've put into trusting God with some of the dreams that I have in these different areas.

With every choice that I make, I try to pass it through the filter of "does this honour God". By no means does every decision I make honour God in the right way, however, my reason for doing so is because throughout my walk with God I've come to the realisation that in order for me to do anything that is truly meaningful in this life, I need him. I sometimes doubt whether I can be someone of good character. I sometimes doubt whether I can be someone that doesn't give in to the temptation to live a double life.

I sometimes doubt whether I can be someone that overcomes obstacles that try to derail me from trusting God...

I know that the God I serve can, and still does miracles to this day, yet I still tend to doubt whether I am actually good enough to live up to all He has called me to. The only way I would achieve true success in life, would be by allowing God to work through me and not doing things purely by my own strength and will. How then, does it make sense that I still question whether I truly have the capacity to not give into life's temptations and trust God, when it would be God preparing the way and not me.

Understanding and internalising the world

When it comes to how we process information, one can either be an external processor or an internal processor. Internal processors are people who like to spend time alone with their thoughts before coming to a final conclusion on an outcome, while external processors talk to think. This means that when it comes to understanding things, they like to get their thoughts out of their head. I see myself as an external processor.

Journaling on a daily basis really helps me to understand and internalise the world. I can recall many a time where I have sat with a friend, rambling on about the many things that tend to disrupt the peace in my life, only to then come to my own conclusion without them having uttered a single word. I'm grateful that the people around me have such patience (and self-control!).

As I began to step out of my teenage years, I remember on at least two occasions, jokingly having a go at my Dad for not showing ANY sign of excitement the first time I rode my bike at the local park in the area I grew up in. It was the sort of thing that I would bring up round the dining table as a laugh to deliver a soft punch that was only just below the belt. I remember bringing it up again after a while, wondering if he remembered the whole encounter at all. He said he did and that he felt guilty about it from the very first time I mentioned it to him (sorry Dad). This was something that happened when I was 4 years old, yet I could remember the exact route I was taking around the park, exactly where my Dad was when he saw me pedalling away like my life depended on it, and his exact response knowing that he knew it was my first time riding my fresh-out-the-Argos-catalogue, orange and black Action Man bike. I remember his reaction clearly. He was walking on the other side of the fence and my recollection of it was that he looked like he was on a very important phone call. We had gone to the park with my mum, so I was over the moon when I unexpectedly saw my dad walking through the park we were at. It were as though the stars had aligned during this moment just so that he could see me riding my bike for the first time. I called out his name saying "Dad, look!" to which he simply gave an abrupt "oh yeah" type of acknowledgement and then continued about his phone conversation in the direction he was already heading in. The more that I talked about it, the more I questioned why this memory out of all my childhood experiences was so vivid in my mind. Then it all made sense; by repeatedly processing it externally, I was attempting to understand a truth about myself. As it turns out, this for me, was the earliest memory I had of simply not feeling good enough.

When I look back on my teenage years, there were definitely reoccurring themes behind the actions that I made. Seeking validation from other people, being one that was fairly prominent throughout. At home I was a bit of a grumpy kid at times, I wouldn't really engage in conversation with people too much unless they really knew me, as I didn't feel as though I needed validation from the people that knew and accepted me for who I was, which at this stage in my life was mostly my closest friends and family. I remember my auntie Shamim coming around to visit us and being so surprised that I said hi to her. When this happened, my sister told me that auntie Shamim came up to her and said,

"Wow, Tendo actually said hi to me!".

There was even another time where I had come back for the Christmas holidays during my first year of university, and I was at a Christmas gathering having a talk with a friend's mum. Whilst catching up with this friend she couldn't stop expressing how surprised her mum was that she had a full on back and forth conversation with me. Upon reflection, these were moments that I could see the impact that my desire for external validation was having on me. It was putting limitations on how I expressed myself, to the point where I can recall being in the park with some of my family and friends and my Dad seeing me swinging on a set of monkey bars and saying,

"Wow, Tendo, I've never seen you play before!" (He can be so dramatic).

I chuckle at it but hopefully that paints a bit of picture as to what I could be like sometimes. At the point of writing this, I'm twenty-three years old and for the last three years of my life, I was quite hard on myself for how I was as a teenager. The things I did and the way I used to treat certain people really used to eat me up, but I've learnt to show myself more grace. On reflection, I think that one of the main reasons why I was this way for a while was because I was still figuring out how I wanted to express myself as a person.

I didn't really feel that comfortable getting overly excited about things because I was too concerned about what other people would think.

This type of mindset showed up in me being fairly closed off at home but then at school I would say it was probably quite the opposite. My parents both worked incredibly hard to send me to one of the best schools in my area (Croydon, South London) and whilst I was there, Whitgift School was one of the best sporting schools in the country, producing countless professional athletes in sports such as football, rugby, hockey and cricket to name a few. What this meant for my school life was that the kids who were the best in the year at their sport sat closer to the top of the social hierarchy.

Hockey was a sport that I managed to pick up while I was there. I even got good enough to represent England at U18 and U21 level, including going to the 2015 U18 European Championships held in Santander, Spain.

I can recall one lunch time during year eleven, I was sitting with a group of friends I used to spend a lot of my time with. One of my PE teachers came up to me and said directly to my face in front of the 3 friends that I was with,

"Tendo, stop trying to copy what these boys are doing, you need to be your own man".

His comment was met with an eruption of laughter from my friends and embarrassment from me. We were sixteen years old at the time. An age where a lot of us boys tend to think we are – as us British people would say – 'the dogs bollocks'. Despite this persona I was trying to present, what he said really struck a nerve inside of me. Hindsight is an amazing thing because I can now look back with more of an understanding behind what I truly felt about the things I experienced in the past. Thinking about this comment now still surprises me. I did have some sort of relationship with this teacher, but I wouldn't say it was enough for him to know when I was acting out of character or not. It must've been evident that a lot of what I was doing and the way I was behaving was simply to fit in. Without him knowing, he stabbed right into the heart of a deep insecurity of mine – that I wasn't good enough.

During that stage of my life, I chose to seek validation from the people around me by trying to be someone that at the root of it, I never believed I was. I feared that if I allowed myself to be shaped and fitted into the mould that God was trying to build me in, I wouldn't be good enough to be loved by the people that I called my friends at that time. Yes, I had my family that loved me dearly, but I was too blinded to see that. I felt like I wouldn't be good enough to still be someone that other people at school wanted to be around. I felt like the only way I could experience any sense of security would be through me being in with the popular crowd, doing things without any thought, just so that people could say, "Yeah I rate that Tendo guy still".

From the ages of 11-21, the majority of my time was spent playing hockey, with the aim of one day representing Great Britain at senior international level. I was able to share many great experiences with amazing individuals. My highlights included playing in the Premier League in England, being able to represent England at U18 and U21 level at the age of seventeen and winning three school national titles at U13, U14 and U18 level with friends that I still have to this day. But still, feelings of inadequacy were prevalent in this area of my life as well.

If you're reading this, I'm going to assume that you're probably wondering how on earth a black man ends up playing a sport like hockey. For a lot of my friends and family, I'm the only person that they know that plays the sport! Well, it all began for me at the ripe young age of 11 in year six. There was this kid in my class called Charlie Hutton who absolutely loved this sport. Every lunchtime he begged me to go to the AstroTurf with him to play hockey with the rest of the kids in the school that played the sport. Initially I completely dismissed his requests but then one day I said, "Fine! Let me come to one training session". To this day there's one moment from that session that I will never forget. We were in the middle of a training match and to be honest I was just playing based off of my instinct. I didn't expect to do much seeing as this was my first time playing the sport. I picked up the ball in midfield and turned into space so that I could go forward towards the goal and then all of a sudden our coach blew his whistle and said,

"Everyone! I want you to stop right there and look at what Tendo just did!".

He then went on to give a full breakdown as to why the movement I just made was so good and how moving the ball into space that way helps us to make better decisions going forward etc. I was buzzing! I guess that's where you could say my love for the sport began.

Charlie was one of, if not, the best player our age in the country and singlehandedly won us our school national titles two years in a row at U13 and U14 level. He was tipped to go on and represent England at junior international level and on top of that, he was an A* pupil. Unfortunately, in the summer of 2012, he tragically died in a boat accident.

He was one of my best friends at the time and that was the first point in my life that I had experienced someone so close to me pass away. I remember feeling as though there was a legitimate hole in my chest when this happened, as though someone had taken a piece of my heart that I wasn't sure whether I would get back. He was one of the best players in the country for my age group and with his passing, without necessarily vocalising it, I said that I wanted to win at least one more national title with our school team in honour of him.

The year after his death I had been picked to play for the year above me and we reached the national final but lost on penalties. The year after that, we got knocked out in the second round and the year after that, we got knocked out in the quarter final. We didn't get anywhere close to achieving this feat until our final year playing as a team together at school before life took everyone their separate ways. I'll always be so proud of what we achieved because losing Charlie was hard on everyone. We were 14 years old when he died, and I guess we didn't really know how to express our true emotions towards something that was so close to all of our hearts. That season was the most cohesive we had been as a team, we knew that if we were going to do anything memorable that year, everything would need to be done from a place of unity. Winning the national title that year would've been the perfect way to share my last moments in school with people I had been with for the previous seven to eight years. Years in which we fought, laughed and cried real tears with each other. In the end, we lost quite convincingly in our semifinal and I took it as another reminder that I simply wasn't good enough.

At this point, this had become my norm. Without realising, I was beginning to accept that maybe I could do good things, but I didn't have what it took to do great things. However, this all changed for me in 2019.

I reached a point where I was very frustrated with where I was in my life. During my first semester of my second year at Loughborough University, I remember just crying for several evenings because things just weren't where I wanted them to be. My dreams of playing hockey fulltime were pretty much out the window, my academics weren't going great at all and I also wanted one of those "girlfriend" things to ease the pain a little bit! I knew there were things that I wanted to achieve, but I was nowhere near fulfilling some of my goals any time soon, at least by my own understanding.

One of my sisters was part of a Christian society at her university called Radical Youth and each year they would put on this amazing showcase called 'Encounter'. I attended the event in 2019 and I did in fact have my own encounter with God. We were praying together in her room the day after the production and I remember sitting there feeling so fed up. During my teenage years, my relationship with God was pretty "lukewarm". I'd pray only when it was really convenient, and I was pretty much MIA when it came to my church attendance. At age 19, I decided I wanted to change all of that and really take hold of my relationship with God and to be honest I thought that because I made this decision, my life would now progress in a very smooth and linear fashion with all my wishes being fulfilled in the way that I wanted. Go to uni, get a good degree, not face any struggles in anything I pursue, whether that be work, sport or relationship related. This most definitely wasn't the case, in fact I could probably say that the exact opposite of what I wanted to happen in my life was happening. I was angry at God. I felt like he had made all these promises to me and I wasn't anywhere near them.

I sat in my chair and I could feel myself beginning to well up with tears. Now to put this in context, I am the oldest child in my family with three younger sisters. In no way do I like being that vulnerable in front of my siblings as I know that they all look up to me as their older brother, I much prefer to be the one that they feel they can open up to, but I guess it takes two to tango. The tears were building up with full force and just as I was about to tell

God, "I just don't feel good eno…" he interrupted me in a still small voice and whispered into my heart "You are good enough". At this, I begun to cry uncontrollably because I realised that throughout all this time, I had been seeing myself through the tinted shades of my own perceived deformities rather than through the clear lens of my loving father in heaven above.

Before I step into this revelation, allow me to say that God sees everyone through a loving lens, and all can view themselves in the same light. His word tells us that he knows the plans he has for you and that these plans are to prosper you and not to harm you. These plans are to give you hope and a future. (Jeremiah 29:11). This tells me that in his eyes, *you are good enough and are more than capable of becoming all that he has called you to be.*

PART 1

PLANT THE SEED

2

WHO AM I?

"The question of identity supersedes the question of purpose. The question of purpose is all about what you are to do, but once you discover who you are, what you do becomes a bi-product of who you are."

– Andrew Twesigye

For some people, the subtitle of this book may not necessarily meet you with good news. Don't doubt who God has called me to be? What does that even mean when I don't know who I am! No need to worry, you're not alone in this. It's easy to look at someone else and think that they're acing this class called life with flying colours, meanwhile you're just making it over the pass mark each semester. I want to encourage you and say that this isn't the case. Deep down we all have our own uncertainties and insecurities about who we are, no one is THAT good. This is why I place such an importance on getting into the word of God, daily.

Why start with the Bible?

Living by Gods word provides us with wisdom, purpose and direction for our lives. I believe that it's important for us to root our identities in what God has to say about us in his word, rather than the things that we may see portrayed around us in the world.

Questions to do with purpose and who we are, are all existential questions about life that go very deep. Studies in behavioural economics show us that when we are faced with an overload of information, we have more of an inclination to go with what the default option is. This is what economists call the "default effect", the option that requires us not to do anything.

In our society today, I've found that we are made to seem as though we are "less than" if we don't possess some of the material things that are portrayed and advertised in the media. Popularity and prestige seem to act as part of the foundational elements that form the mainstream notions of success that we see in the media today. Without these two things, it's easy for us to feel as though we aren't good enough.

I remember having a conversation with a friend at university who was really passionate about photography and videography. She was showing me all these examples of the type of content that she'd like to create and was describing ways in which she would make it unique to her style, it was all so amazing. I asked her when she was looking to start and she said she didn't want to because she didn't have what she perceived other people to have; the popularity, social status, network etc

The default option in life is to lower ourselves to these standards and simply do things the way the rest of the world does things, being held back by the norms that they set. The problem with this is that if we choose to plant our identity in a world that is so fleeting, we'll eventually choke ourselves up and die. Standards are constantly changing and there's no guarantee that what is fresh and relevant now will have the same value tomorrow, let alone in years to come. In fact, most trends tend to go in cycles. Things that were once fashionable go out of style and then come back ten years later at double the retail price, labelled as "vintage" or "antique".

But the Bible says that, "Heaven and earth will pass away, but My word will by no means pass away" Matthew 24:35 (NKJV). Therefore one thing that will never change is the word of God.

"If you listen to the Word and don't live out the message you hear, you become like the person who looks in the mirror of the Word to discover the reflection of his face in the beginning. You perceive

how God sees you in the mirror of the Word, but then
you go out and forget your divine origin"
                                    (James 1:23-24 TPT)

This passage of scripture in James likens the Bible to a mirror. We all know the purpose that a mirror serves in our day to day lives. We use them to provide a reflection of ourselves as a reminder of what we look like, say, before we're about to start our day, head out, or to just admire God's marvellous creativity (some people more than others!). The Bible works in a similar way, in that it provides us with a *true* reflection of what we *should* look like, how God created us to be from the very beginning.

If you want to gain a truthful understanding of who God has created and called you to be, the first place to begin with is his word. This isn't something exclusive to those that are just starting out in their relationship with God. It is the case for everyone across the spectrum. You may be about to step into a new season of your life, starting a new school, living away from home for the first time or starting a new job. These are all examples of turning points in life where we tend to question what God wants us to do, and who he's called us to be in these new chapters that we step into.

Letting God grow you

I am learning how to see myself the way God sees me. It's a journey that has required me to make certain pivotal decisions along the way. On reflection, I've found that this journey is not so much a matter of knowing the exact *destination* of where God wants you to end up, but rather, knowing the right direction in which he wants your life to be heading in. Once you understand the *direction* that God wants to pull your life in, it becomes a lot easier to discern what is and isn't for you. Along the way you'll be able to gain more clarity on what that final destination may be and find it a lot easier to drop certain things as you continue to progress, knowing that holding onto them will also hold you back from where you're trying to get to.

In many cases, this can look like evaluating whether the type of people you have around you are beneficial for you or not. I've reached points in life where I have had to bring certain relationships of mine into question. Some close relationships that I've had in the past hadn't necessarily been bad in and of themselves, however, I knew it had reached a point where some were stunting my own personal growth and slowing me down from getting to where I wanted to go in life. Getting drunk, engaging in sexual immorality and foul language were most definitely behaviours that I had thrown myself into during my teenage years and definitely wanted to cut out of my life, as I knew that the Bible was telling me that I should choose to set an example for others in my speech, conduct, love, faith and purity (see 1 Timothy 4:12). I knew that the best way in which I could do this was to start with really assessing my inner circle of friends that I spent most of my time with, determining whether the things that they valued truly matched mine. I came to learn that there isn't always room in the car for everyone to go where you're heading!

Now, I am not an advocate for burning bridges with people and I am not a fan of this whole 'cancel culture' that society has developed in recent years. Growing up, a lot of the friendships that we develop tend to happen based on circumstance, which for most people could be attending the same school, living in the same area, doing the same co-curricular activities etc. Despite this, there are certain checkpoints that we reach in life where we must decide to qualify the types of relationships that we have with the people around us, putting more thought into how much time we are choosing to invest in them. The Bible says in Matthew 22:39 that the greatest commandment of all is to "Love your neighbour as yourself". If you know that there are certain friendships in your life that aren't helping you become better and call the greatness out in you, it would be unloving to lead someone on and still have an active presence in their life, only to be distant and not fully present when around them.

This isn't the case solely for us humans, but the same thing also takes place in nature as well. When you look at the life cycle of a tree, at the very start of it, a seed is planted into the ground. One of the reasons why some trees fail to grow is because another seed has been planted too close to it, causing the space to be overcrowded. This leads to both seeds having to compete for the same nutrients that are found in the soil, sunlight and water, and as a result, nutrient deficiencies develop within the plant that limit it from growing to its full potential. Even nature shows that understanding who we are and how we can live up to who God has called us to be, requires us to be planted in an environment with surroundings that can help to cultivate and grow us into the strong men and women of God that we can be. I believe that this is something that should be pursued out of principle.

I was fortunate enough to have grown up in a community where I had a fair few number of family and friends who were within plus or minus five years of my age. When we were all beginning to step into our 20s, my mum threw all of us I guess what you could call a "coming of age" type celebration. It was a really great night and we had several of our parents/aunties /uncles etc talk briefly on adult things like marriage and finance.

Whilst we were there, we all had the chance to hear from the pastor of the church that most of us grew up in or would've at least passed through at some point in our lives, Pastor Lincoln Serwanga from Liberty Christian Fellowship. During his talk he said one thing that has stuck with me to this day. He said,

"The things that we don't pursue by principle tend to catch up with us by crisis".

I had to pause for a moment as he had said that, as I thought there was so much wisdom and truth behind the comment that he had made. Life may be going pretty well for you at the moment and you may not find it necessary to consider all the things that I've mentioned. For me, this is when alarm bells start ringing because I know that as soon as I start to get the hang of things is when complacency can start to kick in.

We have to remember that a tree doesn't grow overnight. You may be waiting with excitement for your tree to sprout, to then finally realise that there were severe nutrient deficiencies that stopped it from becoming all that it could be. Don't wait for a moment of crisis to push you into living and walking in your God given identity!

You may be reading this and thinking you're already in too deep and have completely turned away from who God has called you to be. I thank God that he is faithful and that there is absolutely nothing we could do that could separate the love that *He* has for *us* (see Romans 8:38-39). You may not yet know exactly who you are, but God's word tells us exactly how He sees us and the best place to start is by knowing and being encouraged that you are his child.

One thing that is so amazing about the way God has made us is the fact that we all have our own personal experiences of him and how he shows up in our own lives. When I think about what it means for me to be a child of God, I know that it means that regardless of what I do I am always loved. No matter what mistake I make I'm already forgiven. And no matter how far I go, he always welcomes me back with open arms.

Going to university has given me the opportunity to make some true lifelong friendships, as well as meet many talented people from completely different walks of life. Whilst at university I began to hone in on my craft for music and I found myself spending much more of my time writing my own music or playing instruments.

I have several friends who make music, all to different degrees of reach. I remember a time where one of my friends had released his third music project and it was a six track EP. Now during this particular time period, there was a more renowned artist who would go on Instagram live every Friday morning and review the new music that had been released that week. His live streams wouldn't draw in crazy numbers, but there would probably be about 25-30 people that would tune in consistently. On the week that my friend had dropped his EP, I was incredibly proud of it and wanted this artist to hear and review one of my favourite songs from his project, so there I was going crazy in the comments trying to get this artist to play one of my friends songs on the live stream. He finally paid attention to me and played my friends song next. I immediately jumped straight onto WhatsApp and messaged my boy saying,

"Yooo! So and so is about to play your tune on his insta live".

He played the song and to be honest as soon as he pressed play you could already tell that he wasn't too impressed with what he was hearing, and boy did I feel bad. I messaged my friend afterwards and asked how he was doing and to be honest he hadn't taken it well at all. It cut him deeply. As uncomfortable and harsh as that experience was, it served as an opportunity for me to remind him that firstly we can't go around comparing ourselves to other artists who have been making music for ten-plus years and are signed to major record labels. We were very much in our growing phase at that time and simply making the most of the resources that we had around us. Secondly, and most importantly, it served as a reminder that as children of God, we are called to serve those around us and not the people that we hold in high regard and deem respectable enough to be served (see Philippians 2:3-4). This artist that reviewed my friends song wasn't anywhere near our direct sphere of influence and so it was never really our concern what his opinion was.

Jesus himself tells us that there's a light that shines within all of us that is so unique to how God has made us to be. He says,

> "You are the light of the world. A city set on a hill cannot be hidden. Nor do people light a lamp and put it under a basket, but on a stand, and it gives light to all in the house. In the same way, let your light shine before others, so that they may see your good works and give glory to your Father who is in heaven."
>
> (Matthew 5:14-16, ESV).

How your light shines isn't dependant on the opinions of others, it shines regardless! Jesus is telling us that there's a value that God sees in all of us that he wants those that are around us to see and benefit from, and as a result give glory to his name for it. So be encouraged friend, in light of all of this, through faith in Jesus, you are a child of God.

> *"For you are all sons of God through faith in Christ Jesus." (Galatians 3:26, NKJV)*

3

ARE YOU REALLY WHOLE THOUGH?

"Almost every man wastes part of his life in attempt to display qualities which he does not possess." – Samuel Johnson

As mentioned before, I started playing hockey at the age of eleven. However, I didn't have any aspirations to pursue it as a career until I was thirteen. When I began to pursue this goal, I assumed that this was all that I could and should do; play hockey full time throughout my twenties, retire, find myself a regular job, start a family and live happily ever after. I was under the impression that I could only be one thing and nothing else.

My family is flooded with musicians, my late grandfather Henry Wassanyi Serukenya was a composer, and he did so well to pass down the musical gifts that he had to the generations that came after him. Before I was well into my teenage years I actually had a growing passion for music, I used to have lessons in the piano and guitar and would really enjoy singing and playing other instruments like the drums and bass guitar. Once I started to get recognised at regional and national level for my hockey, I began to identify myself solely by the fact that I was a hockey player. I began to feed off of the reactions from other people when they found out that I had played hockey to a certain level, which made me way too insecure to step out and try the things that deep down I felt God was calling me to do, such as continuing to develop my craft in music, something that I had a genuine passion for. I'd identify this as an area of brokenness in my life because at the root of it, I was being held back from my full potential due to the fear that I had of trying something different to those around me and doubting whether I could really place my complete trust in God in this area.

In order for us to truly believe that we are in fact good enough for whatever it may be that God has called us to, it takes coming to a place of wholeness. Although many people don't like to admit it, we all have areas of our lives where we are broken in one way or another. When I was thinking about what it really means to be whole, my first initial thoughts were along the lines of being content with who you are, you know, "being you". I believe that there is an element of truth to this, however, I have a stronger belief that if you want to understand what something that has been created looks like when it is whole, it requires going to its creator. If we want to understand what we look like whole, we have to look at what God's word says.

As I mentioned in the first chapter of this book, a lot of the things that we experience as we develop through life can really skew our perspective on how things should really be, and they can deceive us into thinking that the way we think about ourselves and our situations is the norm. I believe that being whole means to have your identity rooted and established in everything that *Christ* has done and not what *you* can do.

In the Bible, there was a man named David. You may be familiar with the story of how he managed to kill the giant called Goliath with a sling and five smooth rocks, which is found in 1 Samuel 17. His story is one that really depicts what it means to be whole and what it looks like to place your full trust in God. Here is what went down:

David's people, the Israelites, were at threat of being attacked by the Philistines. Their best fighter, Goliath, was a nine foot nine inch giant, and for forty days he had been taunting the Israelites, saying that if they managed to kill him they would have the right to win the Philistines over as their slaves. He was huge, so, I guess no one could really argue against him having that much confidence in his own ability. Before I even get to the part where David manages to kill him, I want to point out some completely justifiable reasons why David *shouldn't* have decided to fight Goliath. Firstly, he was the youngest out of eight sons. His three eldest brothers were in the army and were present at this war with the Philistines. All David was seemingly capable of, was providing his brothers with food whilst they were at war. Secondly, until this point, he had only ever tended sheep. What could you possibly know about being a man of war when you've been doing 'Little Bo Peep' your whole life? Finally, before he eventually killed Goliath he said that he would cut his head off when he didn't even have a sword! Where is the logic in that?

Here's the difference between David and all the other men that had chosen not to face Goliath. Although there were reasons for David to justify why he shouldn't have fought Goliath, his wholeness was something that came from God, and through this, he was able to kill this ugly giant in his way and save his whole nation from being enslaved. His last words before he killed Goliath were,

> *"All those gathered here will know that it is not by sword or spear that the Lord saves;* **for the battle is the Lord's**, *and he will give all of you into our hands" (1 Samuel 17:47 NIV, emphasis added).*

Deep down, I'm sure that David had a strong conviction that God didn't run out of resources on his production line when he made him! He knew that God made every single part of him with a purpose and that everything he had gone through in the lead up to this moment was God preparing him. The great news is that the EXACT same thing applies to you. God has made every single part of you for a specific reason and there is purpose behind everything that you have gone through. Having a true understanding of this can really help bring us to a genuine place of wholeness in the areas of our lives where we are broken, because we will know that in everything that we face, God has done, will do, and shall continue to use all of it to work together for your good if you allow him to (see Romans 8:28). You may be facing a giant of an issue and see that you only have five stones and a sling, but I dare you to challenge your perspective on your current situation. You will never get to see the full power of God in your life and experience true wholeness if you don't trust him with what you already have, whether big or small. For as long as your hand is closed, it will prevent you from receiving all that God wants to give you.

There are many verses in the Bible that describe how we are made new when we come to Christ. Hebrews chapter 10 describes the relevance and magnitude of the sacrifice that Jesus made through dying on the cross for our sins, with verse fourteen saying,

> *"For by that one offering he forever made perfect those who are being made holy" (NLT).*

In essence, this verse is saying that because of what Christ has done, we are made perfect and whole when we come to him. The chapter doesn't end on this note but rather, we are called to continue to persevere with whatever we may face in life, with verse 23 telling us to hold tightly without wavering to the hope we affirm, because God is faithful and can be trusted to keep his promise. God can most definitely be trusted to keep his promises towards us and there are many different things we can do to help ourselves hold on to these promises he has made for us.

Don't worry

When I was a kid growing up, whenever I approached my Dad with a question that started with "what if", his automatic response would be, "What if the sky falls down". This would be his response every single time I would ask him a question of this nature and to be honest, I used to find it really annoying! Imagine coming to someone with a genuine concern, which around that stage of my life would have been things like "what if I don't pass this exam?", "what if I don't make this team?"

or "what if I don't do this right?". The older that I've grown, the more that I've begun to understand why this would be a response he would give each time I would come to him with my concerns presented in this way.

When we look at this story of my dad and I from a linguistic perspective, we can note that there are several tenses that we use to communicate with ourselves and those around us. Conditional tenses are used to speculate about what could happen, what might have happened and what we wish would happen. In English, most sentences using the conditional contain the word "if", and this is typically displayed in two ways, "what if" and "how about if". For the purposes of this chapter, I'm going to say that there's a good side and a bad side to which we can ask ourselves these conditional questions, "how about if" being the good side and "what if" being the bad side.

Studies show that our brains struggle to distinguish between what is real and what is imaginary. Situations that bring about worry are a good example to look at when trying to prove this. When we are worried, our brain produces hormones like cortisol and adrenaline, however, these hormones are also produced when we imagine situations that are worrying too.

When we ask ourselves a question that begins with "what if", what we are doing is stating a condition and asking ourselves or whoever is listening to consider the possible results. "What if" is mostly used for two things: making suggestions and worrying. This type of thinking can come across as innocent and harmless, as using "what if" allows us to make a suggestion that doesn't sound forceful in any way, because we phrase it as something that isn't real. Things like, "What if I tried a new hairstyle" or "What if I dyed my hair brown".

Note the grammar that is used with the two examples above. The phrase "what if", is being used to refer to the present or possible future. What we're doing is imagining a condition or possible situation, however as harmless as it may seem, we already know that the things that we imagine can have an impact on our emotions and how we perceive different experiences. "What if" type thoughts tend to lean more towards self-doubt and worry, and when we worry too much we tend to have thoughts like "what if this doesn't work out?", "what if they don't like it?", "what if I'm not good enough?". These types of thoughts don't always necessarily lead to positive outcomes.

On the other hand, we have our beloved friend "how about if". We use "how about if" to make suggestions for the present and future, examples could include questions like "how about I try exercising more?", "how about I do something I haven't done before?". The implied ending of questions proposed in this way is "is that okay?". If I choose to do x, is that okay? These types of thoughts tend to linger more towards the optimistic side of the spectrum, pondering on the potential of the fruit that could be borne from a particular scenario, as opposed to being worn down by worry, because what if the sky actually fell down?!

Love yourself (especially men)

This is an important point that I really feel like I need to labour. Ladies, everything that I'm saying will be able applicable to you, however I really want to specifically address the guys that are reading this. A lot of the time when you hear people talking about how we should love ourselves, it tends to be from women addressed towards other women. This makes sense given that statistics show that men tend to have a higher level of self-esteem than women worldwide[1], and a study carried out by Cornell University showed that men tend to over-estimate their ability and performance whilst women do the opposite, when in fact, there is no difference in quality at all[2]. Hewlett Packard were able to show that women will look at the qualifications for a job and consider whether they have 100% of the skills before making a decision on whether they will apply or not, whereas men will apply even if they only have 60% of the necessary skills[3]. The issue here is clearly to do with how women view themselves, hence why the language of "loving yourself" has empowered so many women to see themselves in a better light, enabling many of them to walk in more confidence in whatever it is that they do.

Generally speaking, us men tend to be less inclined to be vulnerable and speak out about how we truly feel. We don't like how doing so tampers with how we'd like to present our masculinity. There is so much emotion and expressiveness attached to the word 'love', and I feel it's for this reason that it hasn't necessarily appealed to men in the same way as it has to women. Traditionally speaking, society has placed a lot of pressure on men to be a particular way, and to suppress certain emotions from an early age through "sucking it up" and "being a man". This emotional suppression leaves many men only being able to express themselves on a binary scale of 1 – 2, 1 being angry and 2 being horny. For many men, emotions like fear and hurt are generally masked in anger, and affection is only able to manifest itself in a lustful approach. Thus, if they want to explore a wider range of expression, they don't have the tools to do so. From my own experience, when I've heard men speak around the subject of self-esteem/belief, the language used tends to include "being confident", "leading" or "growing greater capacity". Yes these are all great characteristics for us men to develop in our lives, however, I think that the issues arise when this is all that men try to pursue. Why? They are all performance related and can easily be faked.

In the United Kingdom, men are three times more likely to take their own lives than women, with the highest suicide rate being for men aged 45-49[4]. You hear about many male celebrities that end up taking their own lives and the first response from the general public is "Wow, they looked so happy". They *looked* happy but it goes to show that a lot of people truly aren't. True love – God's love – is powerful and real, something that can't be faked.

I think it's time that all men and women drop the act and really begin to embrace the idea of learning how to LOVE ourselves the way God loves us. Yes, love yourself.

> "We know how much God loves us, and we have put our trust in his love. **God is love, and all who live in love live in God, and God lives in them.**"
> *(1 John 4:16 NLT, emphasis added).*

PART 2

DEVELOP ROOTS

In part 1, we learnt that planting a seed in good soil is the first part of the process that a plant goes through in order to grow to its full potential. We also learnt that planting the seed of our lives in good soil takes knowing who we are in Christ and understanding that in him we are made whole. The next stage that the plant goes through is developing its roots and this is where the real work happens.

4

HAVE YOU EVER SEEN AN ANT IN THE WINTER?

"Every time you take action that builds your character, you become stronger as a person—the harder the task, the greater the character builder."

– John C. Maxwell

I find that the ant is one of the most fascinating creatures to observe. Their physical size nowhere near depicts their true capacity. Given their size, they work best in colonies that vary from 300 to 2000 per ant-queen. In one year, a single colony consumes over 10 million insects. Technically this means that they consume more meat than lions, tigers and wolves combined! The safety of an individual ant isn't what matters most – the colony is always put first. Within their communities, each ant will disregard its own life and put in its best effort to ensure that the colony has what it needs to survive. In addition to this, their most productive season of the year is Summer.

If you follow the principles in this book, you'll reach a point in your life where you'll begin to truly realise who God has created you to be and you'll start to see yourself the way that He sees you. Let's call this season of realisation, the "summer" of your life. No doubt that this will be met with a genuine sense of joy. However, this is the time where you should be using that same energy that comes from being filled with the joy of God to **develop deep roots**. What do I mean by that? It can be extremely easy to soak up all the greatness that comes with suddenly realising that there is more to your life and gaining a true understanding of the amazing plans that God has for you, but it's not God's plan for you to just live in that moment. He wants to see you grow from strength to strength in your knowledge and understanding of who He is, and for Him to be a firm foundation in your life. This is what I mean by developing deep roots.

When looking at the life of an ant, it uses the summertime to maximise the amount of food that it can store, because the cold temperatures of the winter cause the ant to become inactive. I find the perspective that the ant has towards summertime quite compelling, because in a season where it would be completely justifiable for the ant to want to release itself from confinement and roam freely in the heat of the day, it knows that this is a season to instead prepare for its time of need. Listen to me when I say this – in the summer, work your butt off like it's winter, it's during the wintertime that you should have your gas cylinders all filled up because you have paid the price in the summer of your life. When do ants begin to build their ant hills? In the summer, a season where there is no rain, so that when it begins to fall down, they're sheltered and are able to store their food safely. The winter could be seen as a time of crisis where the survival of the ant is at risk, yet this would only be the case if they had not prepared themselves for this season *during the summer.* In times of crisis, you draw from what you have previously stored, *your* survival is determined by the depth of your roots and what you have deposited in your heart. It's not time to look for water when there is a crisis, it's too late at that point. My question to you is, what have you got in your store?

Learning from our elders

My mum and her siblings came to the UK in the early 90s when she was around sixteen or seventeen years old. The house that they moved into is the house that my grandparents have been living in ever since. I've moved house several times, so I always appreciate when I go to a house where a family has been living there for twenty-plus years and I find markings on the wall or particular items in the house that can be dated back to an awfully long time ago! My family and I lived with my grandparents for five years and just before we moved out,

I remember digging out an old photo album and seeing a picture of two of my aunties in their twenties, standing in the exact same spot that I was standing in. It was such a weird moment for me whilst I was staring at this photo, I was in the exact same spot in the house that they were standing in, and when this photo was taken, they were my age. In this one moment, I was looking at them in their mid-twenties and seeing myself now. I was stunned by the realisation that the same thoughts that I have about my future and where I could end up, were thoughts that they probably had once when they were my age, heck they probably still even think them now in their thirties and early forties.

Growing up, I'm sure that a lot of us viewed our parents or other parental figures as superheroes, as in literal heroes that can't really be harmed by a lot.

When my youngest sister was born, she was diagnosed with downs syndrome, which came as a complete shock to my family and I, as learning disabilities were something that we had absolutely no knowledge on. It isn't until we actually witness these parental figures in our lives going through something difficult that we get shocked that there are things that they struggle with, and that they also need protection just as much as their children do.

Another story that I can recall where I had a similar realisation was when I was in Uganda with my dad in the summer of 2017. We had decided to go on a walk together in a town called Nalumunye, this is where our home is in Uganda. After walking for some time, it had started to get dark and this brought up two really stark differences in emotion between my dad and I. Whilst we were walking, I randomly expressed my amusement at some of the things that I was seeing, and my dad was so surprised. In that moment, he began to explain to me how he was beginning to feel anxious because of what he had experienced in the past, as though he was nineteen years old again. For him, the sun going down meant that danger was near, meanwhile, here I was by his side, nineteen years old, and experiencing the exact opposite emotion, happily jumping in and out of potholes in the road.

I'm grateful for the position that I hold in my life right now. Approaching my mid-twenties, I am in a place where I am able to begin to genuinely appreciate and understand the weight of some of the sacrifices that my parents' generation made to hand us the opportunities that we have today. Particularly because my parents at different stages of their lives decided to move from Uganda to the UK in hope of a better life for them and their children to come.

There is a lot of wisdom that we can gain from those much older than us when it comes to navigating through different seasons of life. As these are people that have been through what we've been through, come out the other end and are able to look back retrospectively and reflect on how they carried themselves during that particular season. A younger me wouldn't have given too much thought to the wisdom that can be gleaned off those that have already gone ahead of us, however I now understand and appreciate their hard work and effort so much more.

Not a lot of us are fortunate enough to have parents or parental figures who act as great role models for us, however I think that we can learn just as much from the mistakes that people have made too. It all goes back to the question I pose of what it is that we choose to keep in our stores. Storing the mistakes that others have made and understanding how you can avoid them is just as valuable as being able to store wisdom from a plethora of positive examples around us.

Going back to our observation of the ant, three core values come to mind – **humility, hard work and honour**. These are values that I deem as vital to ensure that we can grow deep roots that act as a foundation and hold us upright during periods of instability in our lives. 1 Samuel 16:7 says,

*"...The Lord does not look at the things people look at. People look at the outward appearance, **but the Lord looks at the heart**"*

(NIV, emphasis added).

Harbouring bitterness and pride in your heart will only hinder your progression towards where God is trying to take you. I'm reminded of Joseph's story in the Bible (found in Genesis chapters 37-47), the one which Andrew Lloyd Webber composed a Broadway musical, titled "Joseph and the Amazing Technicolour Dream Coat". Joseph was a man with a dream and reflecting on his story highlighted to me how humility, hard work and honour were ever present in his character through every challenge that he faced.

With my own dreams, I have been guilty of deceiving myself into thinking that the reason why I have wanted to achieve them, was so that I could testify of God's goodness to those within my sphere of influence, showing them what you can achieve when you place your trust in God. The biggest example of this was shown within my aspirations to represent Great Britain in hockey. This was a genuine desire that I felt God had placed on my heart, but as the passion for it began to wane and certain milestones that I expected to hit weren't reached, I had to ask myself, what was the reason *why* I wanted to achieve this goal specifically? I came to the realisation that when it came to this dream of mine, I was under the perception that the only way I could be a great example and role model to those around me, was through being on a platform that I thought *others* deemed as credible. This showed me that my self-worth was rooted in how other people would view me. I had an underlying sense of pride that was coated in false humility, wanting to be on a platform that others would be able to see me and say wow, "look at how amazing he is!" and not necessarily "look at how amazing God is!". All of this because I didn't feel good enough? Potentially.

Humility

Did Joseph desire greatness? Yes. Was it something he pursued? No. Throughout the story of Joseph, the Bible says that the Lord was with him everywhere that he went. He was with him as a slave in Egypt, he was with him in the prison cell and he was with him when Pharaoh needed him, which led to him being appointed as the man in charge of the whole of Egypt – a country which was a powerhouse within the world at the time. It's not a bad thing to have big dreams and desires for our lives, but it is important that we continue to keep our hearts in check when it comes to them, to ensure that what we are doing is with a heart that is pure and not for completely selfish gains. With regards to my hockey journey, when I wasn't getting selected for the squads I felt like I should've been in, I got depressed! Why was I allowing something like this to have such a strong hold on me emotionally?

When pursuing a dream, it can be so easy to make the dream an idol. It takes humility to ask God for his forgiveness, accepting that there are areas in our lives where we may be placing certain things above him.

Thankfully, we know that His word tells us in 1 Peter 5:6-7 to cast all of our cares onto him because he cares for us. Casting our cares to God is an act of humility in and of itself. When faced with difficulties in our lives, having the desire to cast our cares to God shows that we understand how great and powerful God is. Casting our cares to God shows that we acknowledge that in order for us to continue moving forward in life we *need* God's intervention and at the right time, He will lift us up in honour.

Hard work and Honour

Joseph desired greatness but he didn't pursue it. To pursue means to follow someone or something, usually to try catch him, her or it. Instead of following his dream, his dream followed him, as he followed God. His heart was for God first and foremost and this was shown through the hard work he put in as a slave whilst working under Potiphar, as well as through the honour he showed to God in the face of temptation.

The Bible says that Joseph was a very good-looking man and had drawn the attention of Potiphar's wife. On more than one occasion, Potiphar's wife literally begged him to sleep with her. Staring temptation dead in the face, he said to her,

"…*How then could I do such a wicked thing and sin against God?*" (Genesis 39:9, NIV). Here's some free dating advice, you can tell a lot about a person through how they initially respond to certain situations! Joseph's response wasn't, "How then could I do my boy Potiphar dirty?" it was "How could I do my heavenly father so wrong?". Arguably the former response would be a legitimate enough reason for him not to sleep with Potiphar's wife, however, in everything he did, he chose to honour God first, before anyone else.

Within his story, he ends up in jail and interprets the dreams of two people that play a pivotal role towards him eventually becoming the most powerful man in Egypt. I'd argue that if it was Potiphar's attention that he was solely after, he wouldn't have given these men the time of day. His mind would've been too caught up in thinking "What can I do to get Potiphar's attention?" that he would've neglected the gift that God had given him of interpreting dreams. Because Joseph chose to honour God first, he recognised that he could still put to work the gift that God had given him, despite not being on the platform that he had once dreamt of. That is a true sign of hard work and honour.

"Go to the ant, you sluggard; consider its ways and be wise!" (Proverbs 6:6 NIV)

5

WHO TOLD YOU THAT?

*"No factor is more important in people's
psychological development and motivation than the
value judgments they make about themselves."*

—*Nathaniel Branden*

Bryan Stevenson is an American lawyer, social justice activist and law professor at the New York University School of Law. In a TED Talk he gave on injustice, he spoke about the importance of identity and shared a story about a conversation between him and his grandmother. He described the story like this:

"She sat me down, looked at me, and said, 'I want you to know I've been watching you. I think you're special. I think you can do anything you want to do.' I will never forget it. And then she said, 'I just need you to promise me three things, Bryan.' I said, 'Okay mama.' She said, 'The first thing I want you to promise me is that you'll always love your mum.' She said, 'That's my baby girl, and you have to promise me now you'll always take care of her.' Well I adored my mum, so I said, 'Yes mama. I'll do that.' Then she said, 'The second thing I want you to promise me is that you'll always do the right thing even when the right thing is the hard thing.' And I thought about it and I said, 'Yes, mama. I'll do that.' Then finally she said, 'The third thing I want you to promise me is that you'll never drink alcohol.' [Laughter] Well I was nine years old, so I said, 'Yes, mama. I'll do that.'"

When he was around 14 years old, Bryan Stevenson found himself out in the woods with his older brother and sister. His older brother had bought some beer and was trying to get him to take some, but he wasn't feeling too good about doing that.

"And then my brother started staring at me. He said, 'What's wrong with you? Have some beer.' Then he looked at me real hard and he said, 'Oh, I hope you're not still hung up on that conversation mama had with you.' [Laughter] I said, 'What are you talking about' and he said, 'Oh mama tells all the grandkids that they're special.' I was devastated. [More laughter].

Stevenson then went on to say, "I'm going to tell you something I probably shouldn't. I know this might be broadcast broadly, but I'm fifty-two years old and I'm going to admit to you that I've never had a drop of alcohol. I don't say that because I think that's virtuous, I say that because there is power in identity. When we create the right kind of identity, we can say things to the world around that they don't actually believe makes sense. We can get them to do things that they don't think they can do."

Self-Reflection

Having the ability to self-reflect is an important part of being able to grow and develop as an individual.

Gestalt therapy is a form of psychotherapy that looks to help individuals deal with the challenges that they are facing in their lives right now and not what they may perceive to be happening based on past experience. According to 'Psychology Today', good candidates for gestalt therapy are "those who are interested in working on their self-awareness but may or may not understand the role they play in their own unhappiness and discomfort".

Within every interaction that we have with people, different emotions are being projected through our body language, the words that we say and how we respond to the things that are happening around us. Us as human beings can have a tendency to project emotions that we can't own ourselves onto other people, as a way of avoiding the hurt that may come with having to deal with some of the deep rooted issues that we may be facing. This is called 'project identification'.

The best example to help illustrate this concept is that of a baby. A child has a tendency to hold its environment responsible for the emotions that develop inside of itself. The child who projects will hive off unwanted attributes onto others, making others responsible for feelings and attitudes which in fact are part of itself (O'Leary, 1992: 41). As much as you may be reading this as a full-grown adult, I'm sure that many of us can confess to times that we've had our own (occasional) 'infantile' outbursts, showing that this notion of project identification isn't something that feathers with age!

One way in which I believe we can combat negative emotions and feelings that we've mistaken to be a part of our identity is through asking ourselves this simple question. Who told you that? Now, it may not be a particular individual that has said something that has directly spoken to an insecurity of yours, you may have an amazing support network around you. I've found that in my own case, having great support hasn't been something that has made me exempt from feeling insecure and not good enough in different areas of my life.

We all know how much of a role the internet and social media play in the society we live in today. When used wisely, social media can be such a great tool for building business, developing connections, ministering to and encouraging others without having to be with them physically. However, the internet also gives voice to many people that have absolutely nothing good to say. Social media in particular has its way of giving these same people unmerited access to your thoughts. Think about it, every message that you receive on your smart phone or tablet triggers a thought, whether consciously or subconsciously. Every decision we make stems from a thought and going by this reasoning, we must be sure to always question who or what is dictating the decisions that we are making. The things we consume, the things that we feed our minds with have a huge impact on the story that we tell ourselves when we experience different things in life.

Vice or Virtue? The choice is yours

Vice, according to the Collins English dictionary is defined as "a habit which is regarded as a weakness in someone's character, but not usually as a serious fault." In the society we live in, a lot of our culture is rooted in vice, sarcasm, a type of put down culture that subtly lets other people know, "I'm better than you". I've found this particularly true in contexts that are competitive by nature.

I understand that within a lot of us, we possess a desire to win and succeed at something that we may be pursuing. This could include getting a call to play at a big music gig, receiving recognition for your positive efforts at work/school or reconciling a broken relationship. In order for us to begin to change the internal dialogue that we have with ourselves, we need to start with considering some of the consequences of our own actions. With a "put down" culture being so prevalent within our society, it can be very easy for us to begin to give in towards the type of behaviour patterns that come alongside giving in to this type of culture, especially when we have reached points of personal success in our lives.

I remember being at university and watching a hockey match with a couple of my teammates at the time. The sun was out and all of us were in good spirits as the game was going on. In this type of context, its generally seen as standard procedure to throw jibes at those playing, all in the name of jest. I remember shouting to one of my friends on the pitch who was wearing shorts, "Have you skipped leg day!". It would be easy for one to see this as a throw away comment, however, this comment was directed towards someone that I had been training with in the gym, someone with whom we'd both been open to each other about our fitness and sporting aspirations. Being in crowds can bring about a diminished sense of personal responsibility to stand by the morals, values and principles that we set for ourselves. Given that hockey was something that we were both deeply passionate about at the time, for all I know, a comment like that could've easily disheartened him and any optimism he had towards himself and how his training had been going.

Imagine leaving a small piece of waste underneath your sofa for a while, let's say it's a drink you spilt and forgot to clean up properly. After a while you go back to clear it up and you find that not only has the liquid dried up and stuck to the floor, but it has now attracted a whole array of ants and an excess of bacteria. You can't be surprised about what you see when you go back to clear it up, only to then find that it has now appeared to present itself in a form completely different to the state you left it in, thus requiring you to gain further support or tools to help get rid of it. Tools and support that may not have been necessary if dealt with in the first place or initially avoided. In the same light, when looking at the comment I made in the context of the relationship that I had with this individual, all it does is continue to pour into the pool of negative stories that we tell ourselves and those around us; making small issues greater and more difficult to cope with.

It all starts with you.

As opposed to pandering to this type of culture, I want to encourage you to choose to live up to a higher benchmark. Let us be conscious about the standards that we set for ourselves and intervene early when we notice a small habit or chain of thought that isn't helpful for us. Let us live by virtue and set a foundation of moral excellence that chooses to bring others up, because society puts us down enough as it is!

One of my favourite verses in the Bible says,

> *"Love one another with brotherly affection. **Outdo one another in showing honour"***
> *(Romans 10:12 ESV, emphasis added).*

The reason why this verse speaks to my heart so much is because whilst everything that we see in society tells us to "win at all costs", the Bible tells us that honouring others is what we should strive to thrive in. Christ already holds the number one spot, and no one will ever take that position away from him, so the best we can do for ourselves is encourage and support each other to keep progressing and moving forward in the lives that he's called us to live. 1 Corinthians 12:12 says,

"The human body has many parts, but the many parts make up one whole body. So it is with the body of Christ" (NLT).

If we, his people are all part of one body it would be a logical necessity to agree with the fact that the choices that one person makes can have an impact on the whole body. God has blessed us all with personality traits, and innate skill sets that are uniquely purposed for the positions he will place us in life. I'm sure we're all familiar with the age-old trope that tells us to "stay in your lane". My main issue with the way people tend to present this message, is that it is seldom stated with a heart of encouragement but rather with a tone of limitation.

As I've mentioned already, I was able to have a pretty successful hockey career during my time as a schoolboy, however when I first started playing I was very awkward! Hockey is such a unique sport because a lot of the game is to do with how you control the ball with your stick. Sports like rugby and football are much easier for people to get a grasp of initially as many people grow up kicking and catching balls from an early age. I remember playing in a hockey match at school and at this point I think I had only been playing the sport for about a year and a half. At one point in the game I tried out a new skill that I was very much developing at that point in time, and I wasn't able to execute it the way that I had envisioned it.

As soon as I tried it, I heard my coach shouting towards me from the touchline,

"Tendo, know your limits!".

It was a very funny moment looking back, however, if we want to change the stories that we tell ourselves then we must also contribute to creating environments around us that go against the norm of the narrative that society portrays. If you have an extremely competitive nature, as opposed to using it to solely get one up on those around you, channel that same energy into putting your best efforts to call those around you higher. As opposed to limiting others to *staying put* within their lanes, we should be lifting each other up to *stride forward* in the lanes God has blessed us with!

> *"How strange a body would be if it had only one part! Yes, there are many parts, but only one body. The eye can never say to the hand, "I don't need you." The head can't say to the feet, "I don't need you." In fact, some parts of the body that seem weakest and least important are actually the most necessary. And the parts we regard as less honourable are those we clothe with the greatest care. So we carefully protect those parts that should not be seen, while the more honourable parts do not require this special care. So, God has put the body together such that extra honour*

and care are given to those parts that have less dignity. This makes for harmony among the members, so that all members care for each other. If one part suffers, all the parts suffer with it, and if one part is honoured, all the parts are glad."

(1 Corinthians 12:19-26 NLT)

6

FAITH IT TILL YOU MAKE IT

"They told me fake it till you make it,

forget that I'll never fake it till I make it, I'll faith it till it I make it.

I've been patient still I'm waiting,

for the day my boat is sailing to a better place, I'm kinda in my second phase.

My saviour he was born up in a manger, so I'm used to small beginnings, but still I pray for better days…"

– Guvna B

During my family holiday to Uganda in 2015, I had gone to do some work experience with one of my uncles who is a journalist out there. We were there throughout most of August and in the UK, this is a time when GCSE and A-Level students get their exam results. I was due to receive results on the 13th of August that year but due to the time difference between Uganda and the UK, it meant that I wasn't going to receive my results until the afternoon, as opposed to waking up straight away and finding out what I got.

To be honest, as I sat in this office all morning, my mind wasn't focused one bit on what it was that I was working on during that time. I was literally thinking, I need 12pm to come so that I can get my results. I attended Whitgift School in South Croydon and for students that were studying A-Level subjects, their criteria was that students needed at least 3 C's at AS Level to move on from year 12 to year 13 (this was before all A-Level exams in the UK were sat at the end of year 13). 1pm came and I remember standing in the bathroom of an office building as I was calling in from abroad to find out what my results were (if you're a student, trust me, it makes your life a whole lot easier actually being in the country you studied in when trying to get exam results).

The woman working at the library picked up the phone, asked for my name and began to read out my AS results.

"Business Studies…C" she said.

"Not the best of starts" I thought to myself, but it wasn't enough to knock me down completely.

"Maths…D". Snap.

"Philosophy…C". Erm, okay.

"Physical Education…E". Cue several words of profanity (I wasn't really on this whole God thing too much back then!).

The outcome of my results meant that I was no longer able to progress onto the next academic year. Looking back, I laugh at this whole experience, but I remember my seventeen-year-old self thinking that I had literally thrown my life away. I couldn't think of anything worse than getting kicked out of school due to lack of academic attainment. This was probably one of the first times in my life where I had to trust God with something that had quite drastic implications for where my life could potentially head. I had to put my faith in him. I was dreading to tell the news to my parents as I guess I just really didn't want them to be disappointed with me. I called my parents and to my surprise they were really supportive and encouraging towards me. They came over to the offices that I was working at and to be honest, I could barely muster up the words to say to them without coming to tears. In that moment where they were consoling me, an old school friend of my dad was walking by and noticed us. He was clearly surprised to see my dad but even more so, he said he had seen a lot online about how I had been playing for England U18s that summer and that I had just been called up to the U21s squad. He was really impressed and proud in-fact and that was a real silver lining in that moment for me.

Upon returning to the UK, I had actually found another sixth form in which I had enrolled at and was ready to begin studying at in September of that year. By the grace of God however, Whitgift wanted to keep me at the school and decided to offer me a 50% sports scholarship, meaning that my parents were able to pay for my extra year at the school with no additional cost! I took BTEC Business Studies and A-Level Mathematics, getting an A* in Maths and a place to study Economics at Loughborough University.

Studying at Loughborough was a dream of mine because I saw it as a great opportunity for me to push towards achieving some of the aspirations that I had set for myself as a hockey player. By no means at all was I thriving academically whilst studying there and I eventually reached a point where I had to retake two of my second-year exams, with the threat of potentially having my studies terminated if I failed.

Usually most people spend their university summer holidays going abroad, working or just chilling. I decided that if I wanted to give myself the best opportunity of being the best hockey player I could be, I would need to spend my whole summer in 2019 in Loughborough, training for the next hockey season, and that's exactly what I did. That summer I had also started a one-year work placement in the university's marketing advancement team, and I was also using my free time to prepare for my re-sits. I sat my exams in early September of that year and patiently waited to see what the outcome would be. I remember talking to a friend after finishing these retakes, expressing my thoughts and feelings towards studying Economics, explaining how I felt my career passions lied more in something that was specifically centred around communication, but I couldn't quite put a finger yet on what that could've been at the time.

The 20th of September 2019 came round, and I received an email from Loughborough University containing my resit results. I opened the link and scrolled down the page to find a statement that said, "Due to insufficient academic achievement, the Programme Board has taken the decision to terminate your studies". I had been kicked out of school again?! This time the situation was worse because the first semester of university was ten days away and within this space of time I had to make a decision: whether I was going to take a year out of university and decide my next steps, whether I was going to try to retake my 2nd year, whether I was going to change course completely or whether I was just going to drop out of university altogether.

Although this situation was worse than what I had experienced in 2015, I was able to navigate my options through those ten days with such peace because I had this underlying confidence and faith in God. I trusted that whatever the outcome was from the situation, He knew what was best for me. At the point of writing I'm entering into my final year of studying Social Work at the University of East London, and the main lesson that I've learnt from all these experiences is the importance of having faith in God, regardless of what our situations look like.

The more that I grow in my relationship with God, the more I understand about how to *truly* place my faith in him and nothing else. Our actions and thoughts provide a better reflection of what we believe is true, as opposed to our words. It can be very easy for us to claim that we trust in God, yet our actions can sometimes show the complete opposite of what it looks like to really believe that God causes all things to work together for our good (as mentioned in Romans 8:28).

In the Bible, Mark 11 and Matthew 21 tell the story of Jesus cursing a fig tree. Mark 11:12-14 and 20-21 says,

"The next day as they were leaving Bethany, Jesus was hungry. Seeing in the distance a fig tree in leaf, he went to find out if it had any fruit. When he reached it, he found nothing but leaves, because it was not the season for figs. Then he said to the tree, "May no one ever eat fruit from you again." And his disciples heard him say it." (NIV).

"In the morning, as they went along, they saw the fig tree withered from the roots. Peter remembered and said to Jesus, "Rabbi, look! The fig tree you cursed has withered!" (NIV).

What's peculiar about these verse is that when reading this piece of scripture at a glance, it can come across as a rather random and harsh act. Why on earth would Jesus care about a fig tree and why would he bother to curse it? Especially when it's not even the season for figs! To get a true understanding of this scripture, we need to know more about fig trees and their purpose.

[5]During this time, the production of figs was particularly important to the life and culture of Jewish people. The season in which figs grew was a time of great rejoicing because there is a particular fruit that only fig trees produce. There were many different varieties of figs that were grown in Palestine during this time, with the vast majority growing during a particular season of the year. There were some types of figs whose season of fruit bearing came at a different time however. When these types of fig trees brought forth figs outside of fig season,

the fruit that came from them gave the people of Jerusalem a greater level of satisfaction, this was something that they saw as a delicacy. A foolproof method for one to conclude that there were figs on a tree was if there was an abundance of leaves present on the tree.

In the case shown within Mark 11, when Jesus approached the fig tree he found nothing but leaves. The reason why Jesus cursed the fig tree was because that action displayed God's heart towards hypocrisy. The fig tree presented all the external features of bearing fruit, but it possessed none at all. The tree wasn't cursed because it didn't have *enough* figs, but rather because it had none, *yet still put across the impression that it would.*

The phrase "fake it till you make it" is one that has been thrown around for years and years and it's something that has become common for many people to almost live by. Living by the mantra "fake it till you make it" means putting all your efforts into making sure that externally you look as though you have it all together, when inside you're crumbling. Choosing to "faith it till you make it" means accepting that on our own, without Christ, we simply aren't good enough and that through faith in him we can continue to grow into all that he has created us to be. Sometimes this may mean going back to the drawing board and starting over.

I like how Bishop TD Jakes once put it in one of his sermons on growth. Imagine a chart that was numbered from 0 to 100 in rows of 10. As you go down the chart, the first number at the start of each row increases, but after it there is a zero. As we progress and grow through life, no matter what stage we are at, we will always find ourselves back at 0. Remember spending the whole of primary school waiting to get to year 6 so that you could sit on the benches in the school assembly? Only to then find yourself at the bottom of a very steep pile once you step into secondary school. Or how about when you've been so excited about making your own money? Then coming to the realisation that a lot of that money has to go towards a new bill that you have to cover for the first time.

We all go through phases in life where in order to keep growing and moving forward, we need to start over. Growing in our faith sometimes requires us to go through seasons where we are pruned. In an agricultural context, to prune is to "trim by cutting away dead or overgrown branches or stems, *especially to encourage growth*". To further elaborate this point, it's found that pruning in summer tends to restrict growth, whereas pruning in winter tends to promote growth. How interesting that being pruned by getting rid of distractions that stunt our growth (a process that can be very painful), in a season where our surroundings are already cold and harsh, can sometimes be the best way for us to grow. I know that there are many challenging situations that we can face in life and by no means is it easy to navigate through certain seasons in life, however, I'm adamant that for whatever it is that you may be facing right now, God has given you the grace, courage and strength to get through it.

Shadrach, Meshach and Abednego are great examples in the Bible of people who had complete trust and faith in how God would deliver them. These three men were summoned to be thrown into a blazing furnace of fire because they refused to worship an idol that one of the kings at that time had forced everyone to bow down to. Sometimes we can put this same pressure on ourselves with regards to how we view our thoughts. It can be easy for us to think that because a particular thought has come across our minds, that we are now obliged to go down that chain of thought and end up in a whirling pool of misery. Instead, like these three men mentioned in Daniel 3:17, we can actively choose to not succumb to whatever pressures are around us (and within us) but instead say that "If we are thrown into the blazing furnace – the blazing furnace of our worries, our doubts, our fears – the God whom we serve is able to save us".

What's incredible about the faith that they displayed is that it was so far beyond what they could see in front of them, they had an eternal perspective on how God will deliver them from what was directly in front of them. This is shown through what they add in addition to their statement, saying,

> *"**But even if he doesn't**, we want to make it clear to you, Your Majesty, that we will never serve your gods or worship the gold statue you have set"* (Daniel 3:18 NLT, emphasis added).

But even if he doesn't, there is a far greater plan that God has which reaches further than overcoming this situation. When Romans 8:37 tells us that we are **"more than conquerors** through him who loved us" (emphasis added), it eludes towards the fact that everything that we do is for a greater purpose. Through Christ, yes we can overcome tough circumstances, but we are *more* than that. After being sent into the blazing furnace, Shadrach, Meshach and Abednego came out and, *"Not a hair on their heads was singed, and their clothing was not scorched. They didn't even smell of smoke!"* (Daniel 3:27 NLT). This is the "more" that our verse in Romans eludes towards. We can overcome and then testify of the goodness of God to others, without even a hint showing what we have been through, that they may be encouraged to go and serve God in the same way.

We're humans, so naturally speaking we have a tendency to want things to happen our way, keeping matters in our own hands, as somehow we believe that as long as everything that goes on in our lives is within our control, we'll be okay. Having faith in God isn't about believing that by virtue of praying for something, the only possible outcome is that God will answer that which we've presented to him in the way that we want him to. Having faith in God is about having a heart of humility towards him and trusting him for who he is. As we humbly come before him in our worship and prayer, presenting our requests to him and submitting ourselves to his perfect and pleasing will for our lives, we can trust that he will forever guide us and protect us in everything that we do and anything that comes our way.

Having faith in God can be hard at times, but his word tells us in 2 Peter 1:3 that

> *"By his divine power, God has given us everything we need for living a godly life". How have we received all of this? The second sentence of this verse gives us an answer by saying, "We have received all of this **by coming to know him**, the one who called us to himself by means of his marvellous glory and excellence" (NLT, emphasis added).*

Through coming to Christ you have received everything that you need for living a godly life. This same piece of scripture (from verse 5) encourages us to respond to this promise and many of the other ones God has made to us by supplementing our faith with virtue... to our virtue, knowledge... to our knowledge, self-control... to our self-control, perseverance... to our perseverance, godliness... to our godliness, brotherly kindness... and to our brotherly kindness, love. This is how we fruitfully grow in our faith in Christ.

James 1:2-4 says *"...count it all joy when you fall into various trials, knowing that the testing of your faith produces patience. But let patience have its perfect work, that you may be perfect and complete, lacking nothing"* (NKJV).

PART 3

FLOURISH

7

THE GIFT VS THE ALTAR

"If you'll focus on your character, God will take care of your reputation"

– Steven Furtick

Whilst carrying out some research prior to writing this book, I asked a few friends of mine this question "If you were to read a book that helps you to pick apart self-doubt and maximise your God given gifts. What would you be intrigued to hear?". More than half of the responses that I got from people included something that was related to identifying what their gifts were. Responses included,

"What are my specific gifts…"

"What different types of gifts there are and how to identify them…"

"Steps to take to maximise gifts…"

"How to access my God given gifts…"

Okay, here is an honest moment of transparency, this was a task that was set by my writing coach and it was very much something that I did last minute and didn't think I was going to get much out of (sorry Roxanna!), however the responses mentioned above did trigger a thought in me.

I've personally found that when anyone talks about being all that God has called them to be, the first place that my mind goes to is that of gifts. The sorts of questions I end up asking myself are, "what am I good at?", "how can I get better at this?" and by the time I'm done, those thoughts tend to morph into, "I'm not as good as them at this", "I don't think I can get much better". Yes it's important for us to cultivate the natural talents that we have, the things that we can say "yeah that's normal for me" to, however I'm a strong believer that these things shouldn't be the ultimate aim for us. Being all that God has called us to be has hardly anything to do with the things that we can do, but rather I believe it has everything to do with who we are.

I remember during the height of the lockdown in the UK in 2020 I was about to start getting back into hockey again, as I had taken a year out from playing. Whilst I was studying at Loughborough University, I was quite diligent with my training schedule which included two gym sessions a week, three on-pitch training sessions and two games a week. The main reason why this was something that I was committed to was because at that time, I had greater aspirations to hopefully pursue a career in this sport. I wanted to try and get back to that level of intensity and frequency of training again. So, on a whim I decided to buy myself a rebound net called a Crazy Catch. I said I was going to get out into my garden everyday and work on my first touch by rebounding the ball against the net and practice my elimination skills at least 100 times each day. To cut a long story short, I ended up giving the rebound net to my younger cousin for Christmas that same year because it was simply of no use to me anymore! On reflection, around that time there was a basketball documentary about Michael Jordan and the Chicago Bulls that had just been released on Netflix called, "The Last Dance", and I think watching this definitely acted as a catalyst towards me purchasing training equipment that I didn't need!

Although I once aspired to play the sport professionally, I had spent a whole season where I had done pretty much no physical activity. The capacity in which I was planning on entering back into the sport was going to be completely different to what it was when I left. It was therefore very unrealistic for me to expect myself to train at the same level of intensity and skill level that I once had when I was training and playing on a regular basis. I would've put myself in a better position to persevere at it if I had taken the time to gauge where I was at, what I really wanted and whether I was still willing to put the work in. There most definitely is a time and place for practice and working on the things that we are good at, however, in my case, my main concern was what I had to do to ensure that this gift I had in hockey would shine in the way that *I* wanted it to, without necessarily considering how God wanted me to use it in this new season that was a fresh start for me.

Aside from playing, I also coach hockey to children from the age of 7 all the way up to 17 and at the time of writing, I am entering into my sixth year of doing so. As an 18 year old at the beginning of my coaching journey, my main concern was getting a decent pay cheque just by standing around and telling a few children to run around a hockey pitch for a day and sign autographs for kids that asked for it! At the beginning of 2021, I came to realise how much value I could add into the life of a young person through teaching them how to play hockey or helping improve those who are more experienced. A lot of this came through reflecting on the time that I spent helping assist my good friend and Great Britain/England international hockey player, Rhys Smith, as he launched his community interest company "Hockey Inner City". A lot of his processes were centred around what was best for the child and their own personal development. As opposed to everything being performance related and trying to produce the next generation of England's best hockey players (which is what the majority of my coaching experiences had been), their main values were centred around work ethic, "racing against yourself" i.e. doing better than your last attempt and not focussing on others around you, as well as informing children and parents of the educational and social opportunities that come from playing the sport. Reflecting on this allowed me turn this experience of mine into insight, and I decided that over the course of the year, I wanted to put more emphasis on ensuring that I got to coach as many children as I could if given the opportunity. I wanted to ensure that each session I carried out was centred on ensuring that the children left feeling a little more independent and confident in their capabilities and who they are. I can proudly say that upon reaching the halfway point of 2021, I was able to coach more than 150 different children! This is a feat that I am personally proud of and choose to celebrate simply because when I had made the decision to get back into hockey after my time out, I wanted to remain on the path of trying to be an outstanding hockey player. Had I been so gripped on holding onto this image I had of being an outstanding hockey player, I don't believe that I would've reached this place that I am at now. Although I most definitely haven't taken my foot off the pedal in terms of my diligence to my sport, my posture has changed. I now see a great opportunity for God to use me through coaching hockey in a way that I hadn't seen before because I allowed God to use this gift he's given me in the way that he wants me to, and not in the way that I solely desire it to be seen.

The heart of the matter

Prior to the covid-19 pandemic and the several lockdowns that took place in the UK, if anyone were to ask me whether I watched TV, my answer would've been no, only because back then I was usually out and about either training, studying or working. However, when you're stuck in doors all day, there's only so much that you can do to pass time! I don't have the commitment or energy to randomly start a series so I prefer to watch films that I know will be done without me being hooked! One of my guilty pleasures are Tyler Perry films (if you haven't watched any of his films, you have a plethora to choose from!).

His film "Why Did I Get Married" is a story about a group of couples who go away on an extended weekend trip each year to spend quality time together and ask each other the question, "Why Did I Get Married". Each couple has their own set of unique circumstance that are displayed and articulated in true Tyler Perry fashion. In the sequel to the film "Why Did I Get Married Too", there is a heightened level of conflict within each couple in the film and there is a scene where one of the husbands ends up in hospital and is on the brink of death. At this point in the film, all the couples have become fed up with each other but whilst waiting together in the hospital to find out if their friend is okay, the wife of the husband who is in critical condition breaks down in front of all of them and cries to them desperately to fix their issues, saying, "Love one another, please fix it, please!". She recognises that what her and her husband have been fighting over throughout the duration of the film amounts to an insignificant value when her husband's life is on the line.

In that moment, she understood what really mattered.

Let's have a look at Jesus.

In Matthew 23 we find ourselves at a point in time where Jesus has just arrived in Jerusalem; the latter parts of his story before he is crucified. When he arrives, he goes into the temple and all these religious leaders try to challenge him and catch him out with the words that he says, but they don't succeed. They leave and Jesus turns to the crowds and his disciples and begins to talk about how lost the Pharisees and religious leaders are in their ways of thinking. This is where we arrive. Jesus says,

"Blind guides! What sorrow awaits you! For you say that it means nothing to swear 'by God's Temple,' but that it is binding to swear 'by the gold in the Temple.' Blind fools! Which is more important—the gold or the Temple that makes the gold sacred? And you say that to swear 'by the altar' is not binding, but to swear 'by the gifts on the altar' is binding. How blind! For which is more important—the gift on the altar or the altar that makes the gift sacred?"
(Matthew 23:16-19 NLT)

There are several things to note. These religious leaders had created a system where they allowed themselves to make oaths that were binding and oaths that weren't binding. Now, an oath by definition is "a solemn usually formal calling upon God or a god to witness to the truth of what one says or to witness that one sincerely intends to do what one says".

Essentially, they had created a system that enabled them to make a promise whilst keeping their fingers crossed behind their backs. Jesus sees that there is no sense in this and poses the question *"For which is more important - the gift on the altar or the altar that makes the gift sacred?"* (v19). As quoted by David Guzik in his commentary on this scripture "Here Jesus emphasised that the altar is greater than the sacrifice made upon it. The altar is the established meeting place between God and man, and our altar is Jesus himself and his work on the cross."

Let's get real

Sex has always been that awkward topic of conversation to have amongst many Christians but to be honest I don't think it's anything that we can and should hide from. Everything that we see in the media today is sexualised. Literally anything from an advertisement of a car model or an advertisement of a chocolate brand. It's sad that even on a platform like Twitter, pornographic videos and images are so easily accessible without any filter or barrier. Around the time where I was getting back into hockey, there were also a lot of personal battles that I was having to fight and reflect on when it came to being sexually pure myself. Sex is a gift that God has given us **for marriage,** but at that stage in time there were moments where my mindset approach was similar to that of the Pharisees and religious leaders that Jesus speaks of. My approach had sometimes been, "I'll make this promise not to have sex, I'll make this oath, but I'll get as close to that boundary as I can – so long as I'm focussed on not having sex!". In my own situation, this piece of scripture posed the question for me, what is more important, sex (the gift on the altar) or God (the one who makes the gift sacred).

The reason why highlighting this is important is because there are areas of our lives where we can identify that God has given us a gift, and it can be easy for us to place more of an emphasis on honouring this gift more than we honour our God who gave us the gift.

Any football fans that avidly watch the Premier League will remember a footballer named Adam Johnson who played at Manchester City and Sunderland. He was a winger who was pretty effective for the teams that he played for and even managed to earn a call up to the England squad and get himself several senior international caps during the time that Fabio Capello was managing the squad. In 2014, at the age of 27, he began to communicate with a 15 year old girl over social media whilst his partner was pregnant, which led to an incident where they ended up meeting up and kissing. Following this, he was sentenced to 6 years in prison for grooming and sexual activity with an underaged girl. Yes, he was a very gifted footballer but now if you say his name, this is the first thing that comes to mind. I often forget to remember that he was also part of the Manchester City squad that won their first Premier League title in 44 years, with Sergio Aguero scoring a last minute winner in what will go down as one of the greatest sporting moments in history. This was someone who, two years prior had been crowned with the reward of being part of the best team in the country, only to have all of that brought to nothing due to him abusing his gift.

I always find it really hard when I see people in the limelight who face scrutiny due to a lack of character and integrity. When these sorts of situations happen, I always do my best not to cast judgement only because I know that I am in no way shape or form exempt from making the same mistakes, we are all human. This is why I believe it's important that we pay real close attention to the values that we stand for and who we are as people. A younger version of myself used to have a mindset of "that could never be me!", but who am I to say that if I found myself in a compromising situation and was in the face of temptation, that I wouldn't fall short.

I say all of that to say this. Don't worry about how well you can do something or how your talents and abilities fair up with someone else's. Being all that God has called us to be has so much more to do with *where* are our hearts are, rather than *what* our gifts can do.

> *"Put your heart and soul into every activity you do,*
> *as though you are doing it for the Lord himself and*
> *not merely for others"*
>
> *Colossians 3:23 (TPT)*

8

DON'T BE AFRAID; JUST BELIEVE

"Worrying is carrying tomorrow's load with today's strength – carrying two days at once. It is moving into tomorrow ahead of time"

– Corrie ten Boom

Towards the end of Mark chapter 5 we meet a man named Jairus who was the leader of the local synagogue at the time. Jairus saw Jesus and fell at his knees asking him if he could heal his daughter who was dying. Jesus agreed to help Jairus and on their way to his house, Jesus overheard some people saying to Jairus, "Your daughter is dead, why bother the teacher anymore?" (verse 35). His response to what he heard, was to turn around to Jairus and encourage him saying, "Don't be afraid; just believe" (verse 36).

In a time where this synagogue leader's environment was giving him all the right signs to be fearful and anxious, Jesus told him not to be afraid but to **just believe**. Jesus knew that he had the capability to raise this man's daughter from the dead and all that he asked from him was to believe in him. What does this mean?

It doesn't mean trying to believe and be afraid at the same, it doesn't mean trying to believe and figure it all out, it means just believing[6].

I remember one of my pastors saying in a sermon, "What would've happened if you stayed at home and blamed God? Nothing! Keep showing up!".

Continuously showing up when called to place our hope in God is something that is never done in vain. Trusting him with the desires of our hearts will always bring about good fruit in our lives. When it comes to our dreams, I want to remind you that you're never too old to start again. Don't be afraid; just believe!

It's never too late

I'm always moved in a different way each time my dad shares his story of how at the age of thirty-six he decided to go back to college to study with sixteen and seventeen year olds, so that he could work towards gaining a degree in Pharmacy and become a Pharmacist. This was a decision that he made when he was flourishing in his engineering career, yet he still knew there was more for him elsewhere. Whenever I hear him tell this story, he always places an emphasis on the fact that throughout this whole process he went through of starting again and pursuing this goal of his, his mind was always focussed on where he wanted to go, not on what he didn't have. Focussing on the latter will only bring about fear in our lives, and faith and fear simply don't work together. We need God in our lives to help us get through the hurdles that try to stop us moving forward. Understanding our need for him and believing in him can only help us to accomplish the things that we once thought were impossible. Don't be afraid; just believe.

We read of all these stories in the Bible of great people, including Abraham and how God promised him and his wife Sarah a son when they were both above the age of ninety! We can very easily become detached from the fact that these were very ordinary people just like you and me, and I mean, having a child at that age just sounds painful! Hebrews 11 details great examples of people who did notable things in the Bible but explains that they were driven by their faith and belief in God, not their fear of what would happen. Imagine how disheartening it must have been to navigate through that on a daily basis. It's not like Abraham was in his twenties, newly married and raring to go. If God had told him and Sarah that they were going to have a child during that stage of their lives, I wouldn't have been surprised if Abraham's response was,

"Well you ain't gotta tell me twice!".. But Abraham was one hundred years old and Sarah was ninety. All jokes a side, these were completely unrealistic physical demands that were set on them, to expect a couple of this age to conceive a child. Nonetheless, this was a promise that God had made to the two of them and they both chose to believe. Hebrews 11:12 says *"And so a whole nation came from this one man who was as good as dead – a nation with so many people that, like the stars in the sky and sand on the seashore, there is no way to count them."* Isn't that beautiful, Abraham, a man that was as good as dead, with the help of his wife Sarah, was able to create a life that went on to grow into a whole nation. Jesus was once a dead man but through his resurrection we now have life and life in abundance. You may feel like your hope for whatever you're facing right now is dead, but God can restore and bring life back to your situation. Don't be afraid, just believe.

It's already done

Matthew 8 and Luke 7 tell the story of how Jesus was marvelled by the faith of a centurion who asked him to heal his servant who was paralysed. The main reason why Jesus was marvelled by the faith of this centurion is because of the response that the centurion gave when

Jesus said that he would come and heal his servant. The centurion responded by saying,

> *"Lord, I am not worthy that You should come under my roof. But only speak a word, and my servant will be healed. For I also am a man under authority, having soldiers under me. And I say to this one, 'Go,' and he goes; and to another, 'Come,' and he comes; and to my servant, 'Do this,' and he does it"*
> *Matthew 8:8-9 (NKJV).*

In verse 13 Jesus says in response,

> *"'Go your way; and as you have believed, so let it be done for you.' And his servant was healed that same hour" (NKJV).*

I love the authority that Jesus makes this statement with, "Go your way; and as you have believed, so let it be done for you".

Another time in the Bible that we see a similar phrase being used is found right at the beginning of the book itself. It's helpful to note that the Old Testament was originally written in Hebrew whilst the New Testament was written in Greek. When trying to get a richer understanding of scripture, it can be valuable to find out the literal Greek and Hebrew translations of the words that are being said, and thanks to technology this is something that can be easily done through the help of online concordances. The Greek word that Jesus uses here for "let it be" is "genētheto". When translated into Hebrew, we get the word "yehi". "Yehi" meaning, "let there be". The same word that God spoke at the very beginning when He was creating the heavens and the earth, He said,

"Let there be" and there was (see Genesis 1).

The Latin translation of this word is "fiat" which according to the Merriam-Webster dictionary means, "a command or act of will that creates something without or as if without further effort, an authoritative determination, an authoritative or arbitrary order".

As much as that is quite a lot of information for one to get their head around, I believe that it does add a lot more weight and insight to the power that Jesus displayed when making this statement. To create something without further effort implies that it is already done. Everything that needs to be done prior to it being brought into existence, prior to it being manifested has already been completed. Jesus was moved by the faith of the centurion and therefore brought into existence what was *already* done.

The centurion was aware of this principle probably more than he even knew, let's go back to what he says in Matthew 8:8-9

> "...***But only speak a word***, *and my servant will be healed. For I also am a man under authority, having soldiers under me. And I say to this one, 'Go,' and he goes; and to another, 'Come,' and he comes; and to my servant, 'Do this,' and does it" (NKJV, emphasis added).*

He knew what it meant to live under authority. If he were to tell someone who hierarchically was positioned underneath him, they would begin to prepare themselves so that whatever request that was made towards them was brought to completion.

The centurion took this same principle but knowing and understanding who Jesus was and the power he had, he acknowledged that whatever came from His mouth would come to pass. He didn't even need Jesus to lay hands on his servant, he understood the power, the life-giving power, of God's word.

Stepping out and trying something we haven't done before is hard! Committing ourselves wholeheartedly to a dream comes with its challenges! In the world of personal development and self-help, talk of pursuing our goals is presented in such a flamboyant way with so much enthusiasm and energy, almost as though to psyche people up into taking that giant leap of faith, but what happens after that? You probably hit "E" (empty) on the tank, burnout and go back to square one, only to repeat the whole process again. When following Jesus' example, he peacefully tells us not to be afraid but to only believe in him, because what he has said has already been done.

I leave you with this:

God sent his only son Jesus to take on our sin and die for us so that we may live for him eternally.

God has given us everything that we need to live our lives for him and whilst we are still blessed with life on earth, placing our trust and hope in him is what helps us grow into the best representation of ourselves.

It's *never* too late to turn him, he sees you – flaws and all, loves you and only desires the best for you.

Stay by His side and you'll lack nothing,

because with everything that you have right now, good and bad, He sees it as good enough to live up to all He has called you to be.

NOTES

1. www.apa.org SELF ESTEEM GENDER GAP MORE PRONOUNCED IN WESTERN COUNTRIES

2. www.theatlantic.com THE CONFIDENCE GAP. Article by Katty Kay and Claire Shipman

3. www.forbes.com THE CONFIDENCE GAP IN MEN AND WOMEN: WHY IT MATTERS AND HOW TO OVERCOME IT. By Jack Zenger.

4. www.samaritans.org

5. www.ligonier.org THE CURSE OF THE FIG TREE. A sermon by Dr.R.C.Sproul.

6. https://www.blueletterbible.org/Comm/guzik_david/ StudyGuide2017-Mar/Mar-5.cfm

Printed in Poland
by Amazon Fulfillment
Poland Sp. z o.o., Wrocław

87796460R00070